MOVING
beyond
TECHNIQUE

MOVING
beyond
TECHNIQUE

how to nurture your passion,
master your craft, and create
a thriving Pilates business

by Chantill Lopez

Published by Chantill Lopez, Sebastopol, CA
Second Edition, 2015

ISBN-13: 978-0-9909088-2-1

Printed in the United States of America

Photography by Amber Weir, Weir Photography and Design
www.wdnphoto.com
Book Design by Patty Holden

WHAT PEOPLE ARE SAYING ABOUT
MOVING BEYOND TECHNIQUE
AND THEIR WORK WITH CHANTILL LOPEZ

"*Refreshingly honest, authentic and inspiring. Chantill, and her ultimate guidance in this powerful book, is the voice that yoga and Pilates teachers have been searching for...even if they didn't know it. Teachers: For your students and your own inner peace, read (and do) this book. It will make a difference.*"

—CORI MARTINEZ, ASHA YOGA OWNER, TEACHER
TRAINER AND INTERNATIONAL RETREAT LEADER

"*I have had the honor of taking the Pilates teacher training with Chantill Lopez and am excited to begin my fourth year in her mentoring program. Chantill's authenticity and grace come through in everything she does, fostering the passionate curiosity about the body in motion that is essential to being a good movement teacher. Her mentoring program covers every aspect of teaching from how to teach each exercise and why, to creating trusting teacher/student relationships, to the business side of things. I wholeheartedly recommend her program for anyone that is interested in digging deeper into their self practice and teaching.*"

—TRINITY MINTY, PILATES TEACHER & OWNER,
PILATES TRUE, AND PILATES MENTOR

"*Chantill has been my teacher, mentor, and friend for many years. She is a brilliant teacher of both Pilates and how to be a teacher— two distinct, but overlapping, pursuits. She has coached me on the foundational things, like introducing myself to clients and cueing from multiple perspectives, and on the advanced pursuits that make good teachers great, like finding strength in times of doubt and insecurity and working with challenging students. She will meet you where you are, help you set goals both personal and professional, and guide you in mapping and executing a path forward. Moreover, she'll ask you the tough questions you may be too nervous to ask yourself! I cannot recommend anyone as a mentor more fulsomely than I recommend Chantill."*

—KELLY MEEKER, APPRENTICE TEACHER

"Transferring educational instinct into workable, measurable progress is something Lopez performs brilliantly. Read this book and improve your Pilates teaching and business acumen no matter where you are in your path."

—ANNE BISHOP, ED.M. FOUNDER BODY BRAIN CONNECT

I recently told the studio owner where I teach that I feel like my schedule is busier and people are staying longer because of my work with Chantill. I feel more energized, more focused, and more excited about my teaching! I know it's working. Of course I really want to be the best teacher I can be and that motivation helps, but our work together is pushing me forward.

—AVA MOTTER, CPT, HENDRICKSON METHOD THERAPIST

"Chantill walks the walk, she is a thoughtful, deeply caring teacher whose insights come from fully facing her own challenges and struggles head on and turning them into victories and growth. I know because I've been working beside her for nine years and can't imagine where I would be in my own teaching evolution without her encouragement to continually reassess and her gentle prodding to step more fully into my potential. As I've watched her turn her discoveries into a successful mentoring program and coaching business I've witnessed how profoundly she has affected her trainees, setting them far ahead of those who've not had the opportunity in their movement training programs to delve into these deeper questions making all the difference in establishing joy and longevity in a fledgling career. Seasoned teachers also reignite passion and cultivate greater satisfaction with Chantill's guidance. Listen closely, dig deep!"

—KRISTEN IUPPENLATZ GRECH, OWNER PILATES COLLECTIVE, FOUNDER PILATES HOME PRACTICE

DEDICATION

*To my teachers, all of whom have given me
something memorable and dear in their endless effort
to be better teachers, to shed light on the
potential joy that exists in the body, and
to put something valuable and
meaningful back into the world.*

I am endlessly in their debt.

THERE IS A VITALITY, *a life force, an energy,*
a quickening, that is translated through
you into action, and because there is only one
of you in all time, this expression is unique.

—MARTHA GRAHAM

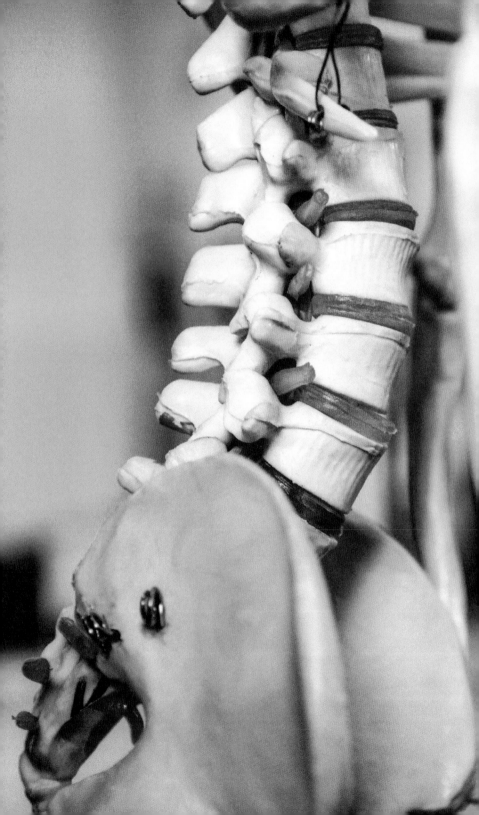

CONTENTS

xii	Meet Your Teacher
1	Introduction
3	How to Use This Book
5	You Are Not Alone
13	What Kind of Teacher Do You Want to Be?
17	Teaching as Change
23	How to Create & Sustain a Satisfying Teaching Life— Five Essential Steps
23	Keep It Simple
25	Create a Vision From Your Core Commitments
29	Always Play to Your Strengths
32	Identify and Face Your Demons, Fears & Motivations
37	Practice Letting Go (and Don't Take It Personally)
41	Cultivating Generosity—The Key to Building a Thriving, Meaningful & Successful Studio Environment
42	Teaching as Service
44	Generosity at Work—Scenarios
49	Taking Student Retention to the Moon—Simple, Actionable Steps to Guide You Now & Down the Road
49	Five Common Challenges in Keeping Students
49	Five Simple Strategies for Keeping Students
59	Five Sure-Fire Tips to Amplify Your Retention Practices
63	Does Your Studio Have Heart?
69	Keys to Cultivating Healthy In-studio Relationships
73	Back to the Beginning: Starting Over
73	What Kind of Teacher Do You Want to Be?
75	Making it Stick
77	Appendix
78	Acknowledgments

MEET YOUR TEACHER

I ride a motorcycle.

When riding a motorcycle there are a few things that are crucial to your success and enjoyment.

The top two in my mind are:

One, a helmet. Two, that you have a riding buddy who loves riding as much as you do — or maybe even more.

Likewise, when diving into this book there are a two things that are crucial to your success and enjoyment.

First and foremost, your protective gear — my contact information.

Cell: (707) 738-7951
Email: chantill@skillfulteaching.com

Second, someone to go on the ride with you — that's me.

And yes, I actually want you to get in touch with me.

Call me, text me or email me. Your questions, comments, and insights are what drive my business and keep me IN LOVE with what I do. You are why I do what I do and I want to help. Without you I'd be sitting at a miserable desk job somewhere having given up teaching for something easier but infinitely less fulfilling, so believe me when I say I want to hear from you. I do!

In fact, while we are at it, here's what else I want:

I want you to KICK-ASS in your teaching.

I want you to not only carve out a long-lasting career, but an entire life that is amazing, fulfilling and sustainable. I want to help you find a way to bridge the gap between work and life so that one is always a reflection of the other: authentic and consistently driven by your deepest desires, core commitments, passion and purpose. It is possible. Teaching can get you there.

So, congrats on picking up this book.

Helmet on. Buddy by your side.

Vroom...

1
INTRODUCTION

IN MORE THAN 15 YEARS as a Pilates teacher, and almost as long as a studio owner, I have learned what it means to work toward mastery. It takes skillfulness to create a joyful and sustainable teaching life, and to discover that at the heart of teaching is a craft. But the path to a highly rewarding teaching life isn't necessarily forged with teacher trainings or even continuing education; it's stumbled upon and learned in real-life practice.

In *Moving Beyond Technique: How To Nurture Your Passion, Master Your Craft, and Create a Thriving Pilates Business*, I pick up where teacher trainings leave off and show you how to evaluate your current teaching life, clearly identify goals for developing your craft and achieve these goals in a manageable way that feels authentic to you. I walk you through how to confront feelings of self-doubt and uncertainty in order to ACHIEVE passionate, inspired and meaningful teaching *right now*.

This book is designed to serve as a catalyst for revitalization. It is a chance to seek, question, and look more deeply into the struggles that we all face in our often isolated quest for professional fulfillment. And it's a tool for feeling supported in addressing those struggles, no matter where we are on our teaching path.

In the **Personal Inventory, Checklists** and **What to Do** sections, I guide you through how to evolve your teaching and business practices, based on your personal core values. These tools offer digestible, actionable steps, and should be used whenever you're ready and at your own pace.

Personal Inventory sections afford the rare, but essential opportunity to pause and reflect. This feature will help you unearth any fears and motivations that you have in regard to teaching and running different aspects of your business. When completing a personal inventory in this book, do so privately, in your favorite cafe or when you are at rest. The benefits of this are twofold: solace will not only provoke the most thoughtful outcome about who you are and what influences your teaching, but will also demand that you make a concentrated effort to nurture yourself—something we all need more of.

What to Do sections are designed to help put your thoughts and any new tools into *action*. In these exercises, you will delve deeper into your personal values, teaching goals, and natural strengths to uncover the steps required to make real change happen, and explore how to enact these changes in your teaching life.

Checklists present new tools, directives, considerations, and ideas for how to get better results for a given goal. These lists will prompt you to parse out a goal into achievable actions. You don't have to do every checklist item in one sitting. Instead, focus on the items which resonate with you most. You will find that different checklist topics will inspire you at different times, so revisit them again and again... and again.

2
HOW TO USE THIS BOOK

YOU CAN CERTAINLY READ *Moving Beyond Technique* all the way through and return to the elements and exercises that feel most relevant to you now. Or you can take a slower pace and explore each section bit by bit. If you take this approach, plan to spend at least two to three weeks on each section. Make sure you give yourself plenty of time to really explore each exercise or topic and create a plan for implementing the tools that will make a difference in your teaching and your business NOW.

Inevitably, each section will have more or less relevance for your particular circumstance; you may find that you spend more time on some exercises and less on others. It's all okay— just enjoy the process. And remember every tiny step you take gets you closer to a more uplifting, authentic and successful teaching life.

I am pleased to offer this introduction to achieving teaching mastery in the non-traditional classroom we call "the studio." And I am excited for what follows…for all of us.

Enjoy!

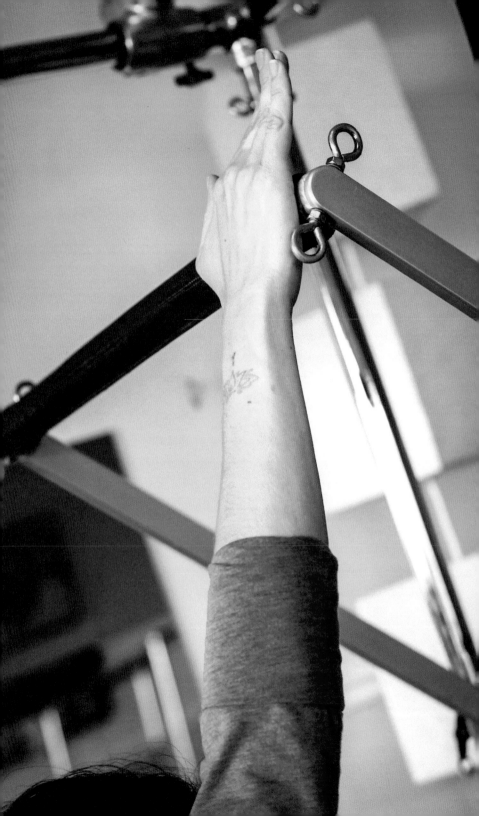

3
YOU ARE NOT ALONE

YOU ARE NOT ALONE. You stand on the shoulders of every person who has ever influenced you in a positive or negative way—every teacher, friend, or passerby that has inspired you to question, reflect, take action, or change course.

More importantly there are teachers like you who also struggle to find rewarding teaching lives, to nurture and share and guide. There are teachers who have the same amazing successes that you have. They wonder how to maintain their confidence and build community; how to share and be a part of something bigger than themselves and the sweaty gym they teach in. (Don't get me wrong—I love sweaty gyms; they are fraught with lower backs that need our attention!)

In this book, I give you key lessons to help you look at who you are and why you do what you do. These lessons contain the most crucial (and often, overlooked) elements of creating a rewarding and meaningful teaching life. I share hard-earned successes, strategies and experiences, gained through 15 years of teaching and a decade of business ownership. These tools and discoveries have made the biggest impact on me personally and professionally and have led me to a successful, fulfilling, and inspiring career; they are also the ingredients that will keep you, the teacher, stable, focused, and able to deal with the uncertainties of teaching, and of life in general.

So, how do we begin? With a surprisingly simple question—and one that I deeply wish someone would have asked me when I started teaching:

What kind of teacher do you want to be?

Now this vital question never occurred to me when I began teaching Pilates at Spencer Health and Fitness in Hilo, Hawaii. The ancient sweat-box was haphazardly adorned with a coat of cheap paint and a few meager single-pane windows. It was no beauty, but it did the trick as far as gyms went.

My first class. I open the door. Sweat hits me like a wall. Walking between rows of Stair Masters, no one knows me from anyone else and I feel safely anonymous. I can hide behind the veil of having no past and no present with these gym goers, relieved that few look up when I pass them on the treadmills. The students are preoccupied with watching Oprah, clocking calories on their digital screens, or mouthing the words to a favorite song.

I walk to the locker room, more out of not knowing where the classroom is actually located—and trying not to show it—than for any real need of the locker room itself. I set my bag and mat down and look around. I simply stand, feeling my heart thumping, the flurry of moths in my belly, my throat lumpy and hard.

Class starts in 15 minutes. It is enough time to get Room A ready for class, but too much time to have to sit there alone, waiting for students to trickle in.

I am filled with a purposeful, yet false confidence; I am wearing my anticipation like an undergarment in snowy weather, hidden and tucked away, careful to not let a thread show. The fear lingering is that of the unknown. As students show up—a grumpy old man, a work-worn mother, an eager gym regular —all seemingly curious but dubious about what the next 60 minutes might hold, I wonder, "Will the words come out right? Do I have a right to be taking this place as expert and teacher? Can I make a difference? Will they 'get it?'" My fear is conjured out of nothingness, like a magical sword with which to arm myself. This is my introduction to teaching.

I had decided, with very little conviction, to be a teacher. I said I would do it, believed in the likelihood of my success and then, at some point, woke up and realized I was doing it. I had become a teacher. But the role and responsibility of being a teacher carried very little weight itself. I wanted to teach Pilates, to move, to share my joy of it with others. I never considered that there might be something more to teaching than simply learning the method and showing up.

I started teaching Pilates as my first real (although self-appointed) role of educator. Today, I teach many things, including yoga, anatomy, meditation, business and marketing skills, how to be an exceptional teacher and a thoughtful technician, how to work with osteoporosis and scoliosis, and much, much more.

I imagine all of us to be teachers at some point, or in some capacity. Perhaps you have experienced the gift of offering and learning as well. Was there a time when you were both the receiver and the conduit of teaching? Was there a moment when you were the supporter and the supported, the questioner and the answerer? Teaching Pilates was my first true experience of performing both roles at once.

My early memories of teaching Pilates are ones of anticipated challenge and unexpected joy. I was endlessly confronted by the inner struggles and questions from my past. Who am I? What gave me the right to be the expert and guide? Why would anyone care about what I was offering? What if I fail, hurt someone, say something wrong? What then? It only took one class, one reality check, before I began to calculate the risks and the possible failures. Soon after, my mind weaved thoughts of grotesque misguidance and ensuing grievances.

It was in my first class in that stale, old gym room, where I was forced to acknowledge the unknown:

Belly down, nose planted into the mat, a student turns to look at me while smashing her cheek to the floor and asks, "What exactly are you asking us to do?" Silence. Um, what? Words lost. What am I asking her to do? With a sudden loss of confidence, I repeat the directions. "What?" she asks again while coming to her knees in order to get a better look at me. I suddenly feel as if I'm sitting bound to a chair in a dark room with a single blaring light on my face as means of intimidation. I would give her what she wanted if I had it to give, but I don't have the answers, and I can't say so.

In Buddhism there is a concept called Beginner's Mind. It is the notion of being able to stay in a humble place of not-knowing, willing to see the open field of possibilities even when they go against what you think you know. In Beginner's Mind you are not fixed or trapped by what you have learned or what you have not learned. When we choose to be untethered by our beliefs or stories—those questionable truths we tell ourselves to justify, reconcile and piece together our experiences—and be open to what's in front of us, there is relief.

An entirely different feeling arises, however, when one is being nudged into this place by someone else. When teaching that first class, my subconscious bodyguard (her name is Ego) had that door bolted and locked. I could not dream of saying, "I do not know."

Instead, Ego was saying, "The first thing you must do is express confidence." Ego crossed her arms firmly and glared. But was I not instilling confidence? Why should I not have all the answers? Was I "allowed" to admit that I did not have all the answers?

So, for the first year of teaching, I simply clutched on to any possible answer whether it was right, semi-right, maybe, sort of right or really stretching it. It was an unsatisfying beginning. Yet, I embraced the reality and moved into the practice of teaching. Swept off my feet like a lustful young lover, I fell completely and blindly into my new craft; I was acutely aware of my lack of mastery but I never stopped to heed it. By a completely selfish impulse, I deemed myself something I had never imagined I would be—a teacher, a guide, an expert.

I have neither an explanation for why I chose to stick with the teaching process, nor will I presume some gifted sense of self-awareness as a reason. While one foot was put in front of the other, trust, faith, and inspiration blossomed under tender ground. And gradually, joy emerged.

For the first few months (and with all honesty into the first several years) there was a constant stream of critical thought, unfamiliar feelings, questions, insights, and intense self-doubt swirling in my head. I held the responsibility to guide and motivate students who put their bodies and trust in my hands.

Could I do it and would I be successful? Well, some days I was successful, and other days I was not. Every moment in class echoed a scratching, scathing voice (Ego's sister, Self-doubt) repeating, "any second now you'll be found out. Fraud! Fraud!" Some days, as a class would end, I would sink into the floor, beaten by all the answers I did not have, the change I could not affect, the body I could not reveal. On those days, I was determined to do whatever it took to become better and stronger.

Other days I glowed, as evidenced by the students purring after class. What a difference I had made: breakthrough, discovery, ease found and restored. I was their guide and reflection. It was light and shadow, reward and payment.

This was the first reflective glimpse of myself —my first gleam of keen awareness, both of my mind and my behavior. Never had I been so aware of who I was, or what motivated me to say the things I said and act the way I acted. I had stumbled onto a road I knew I wouldn't turn away from. I had a sense of purpose and clarity that made anything but forward motion impossible. I did not always like what I saw, but teaching allowed an understanding that there was more to me than I was used to seeing or being. *That* filled me up and it still does.

Equally matched by my inner experience was an outer experience—the one I shared with my students. Had I ever really looked at someone's body and noticed fear in his or her movement? Had I ever considered a student's motivations for being in class, or examined those motivations? Had I asked someone to purposefully and intentionally trust me? The answer is, of course, no—never. And I was more frightened by this realization than any other aspect of teaching. How could I ask for the trust of someone else when I did not trust myself?

The answer? I trusted the process of teaching and learning. It revealed my students' abilities to know their bodies and minds more fully. Witnessing their progress and potential was empowering. I could see that people desired change, and I had come to believe that teaching was more than just repetition and dissemination; it was a relationship. That process has helped me fall into a deeper level of teaching. To witness less pain, greater ease, vitality and strength was (and is) a flame, white hot and singularly focused, that makes my teaching more rich. Week after week of practice has not only led to the opening of students' bodies, but to an expansion of their own self-perceptions. Teaching Pilates has become more than just teaching Pilates; teaching Pilates has presented and opened the doors to unanticipated rewards.

And yet, through all of this, discovery of self and finding the power in the teaching process, there is one thing I wish someone, anyone, would have asked me as I embarked upon this profession. It's a question that could have helped to light my path with more clarity, succinctness and purpose from the get go.

4
WHAT KIND OF TEACHER DO YOU WANT TO BE?

IT'S TAKEN ME NEARLY 15 YEARS to fully realize not only the critical value in this seemingly simple question, but *why* it's a question I had never been asked.

I had an amazing master teacher train me, one who has become a close and valued mentor. She is knowledgeable, tenacious and leads by example. And, she is largely why I know how good it can be to have someone on my side. But the honest truth is, the art and craft of teaching is well overlooked by our industry educators and by us, the teachers, particularly at the outset. Even if we are lucky enough to fully immerse in a program that addresses teaching skills, who will help us determine how *we* (that is, our inner selves) fit into the picture? Who will help us reconcile the teacher within along with the subject we teach? For most of us, the answer is no one. And therein lies the impetus for writing this book.

What kind of teacher do you want to be?

This question is not only relevant to new teachers but veteran teachers as well; it's one that helps assess our path (past, present and future) and helps us figure out where we *want* to go. It calibrates our inner and outer lives and keeps us true to ourselves. It helps us identify our strengths, our gifts and our direction. Without this question we are mechanics without heart, the Tin Man in spandex, lost in a sea of hundreds and thousands of other technicians delivering the same message in the same way with the same mediocre results.

Still there is a greater tragedy: most of us never realize that *we* have been left out of the process of learning to teach. It's not until we feel the emptiness of an unrewarding teaching life, or recognize that something is missing, that we begin to realize that simply going through the motions of teaching doesn't and won't integrate our inner selves and hearts with the outward action of educating.

Where the skills of communicating wisely in student-centered teaching, motivation, non-attachment, self-reflection and personal responsibility can be taught and stored alongside the requisite anatomy, physiology, philosophy and repertoire, oftentimes, it is not. This leaves many of us feeling as if we have some innate professional (or even personal) deficit; it also leaves us with a myriad of questions that arise out of a need to know ourselves better. These questions beg us to look at who we are as people and therefore as teachers.

Questions like:
- Can I be a better teacher?
- Can I be more confident?
- Can I draw students in and keep them?
- Can I be as good as the teachers I admire?
- Do I truly embody my best self when I'm teaching?

- Do I challenge myself by expanding my knowledge of both the teaching material and myself?
- Is my work financially, energetically and emotionally sustainable?
- How do I know?

By taking inventory, reflecting and working on one question at a time, we will begin to know *what kind of teacher we want to be*. Each answer opens the door for us to explore what lies beneath our current motivation and allows us to see ourselves more clearly both as we are and as we want to be.

I invite you to ask the questions that will lead to authentic, meaningful and lasting success as a teacher and see how your answers have the potential to nurture your passion, move you toward mastery, revitalize your students and transform your doubt.

In the **Personal Inventory** sections of this book you will be asked to think about questions relevant to your teaching and journal your answers. Be sure to keep your responses in an accessible place so you can revisit them regularly. Review your answers once every few days to keep connected with your original (and hopefully most honest) assessment and feelings about a particular element of your teaching.

PERSONAL INVENTORY

Getting Started—
Check In with Your Current Teaching Self

This section will help you discover areas of inspiration and discontent in your teaching career, where you have room to grow, and what you're doing right.

1. Do you find yourself feeling at odds with where your studio or teaching is headed?
2. Do you feel at odds with the kind of atmosphere you've created or the teachers you have working for you?
3. Do you feel like teaching doesn't exactly make you feel all tingly inside or do you ever ask yourself, "Is this is what I am meant to be doing?"
4. Are there people (teachers, other staff or students) who you feel are not a good fit for your business or current work environment, but you don't know what to do about it? (Or if you teach in someone else's studio, think about whether you are the right fit for it.)
5. Do you have a vision (even a faint one) for your teaching career, but have found you're unable to implement it?
6. Are your teachers difficult to muster and do they lack interest in participating?
7. Do you find it difficult to stay motivated and participate in your teaching?
8. Do you find yourself working harder and harder, yet not getting the results you really, truly want? ————●

Does any of the above ring a bell? If you've taken an honest account of where you are now, it's likely that some responses to these questions will trigger feelings of frustration or regret. Don't let that stop you in your tracks. You'll also likely see red flags or warning signs, which indicate that something in your teaching life needs to change. If you discover that there is something you can do to solve a problem you have or to bring yourself closer to your teaching goals, then this personal inventory has served you well: take action!

TEACHING AS CHANGE

There is more to teaching then you've been taught. The art of teaching requires more than just knowing your material, finding the right words to move a body or demonstrating proper technique. Teaching is an ever-evolving life-long path of learning and exploration, a personal journey and an opportunity to serve our families, friends, community and even the world. Teaching is leadership, generosity and compassion. Teaching is change!

In my mind's eye I always thought the story of my business would be about how my business partner and I found each other and took a tremendous risk in starting a studio together after only one meeting. It would be a story in which our vision and passion were enough to build a successful Pilates studio— one that was both equitable and creative, and ultimately, the model that others would want to emulate. But it's not that story. At least not entirely.

I don't remember when I stopped enjoying teaching. What I do remember is when I started hating it. I kept telling myself that I needed to cut back my teaching hours because I wanted to spend more time working on the business side of things. At this point, I still enjoyed the entrepreneurship; I was good at it and that's where I wanted to start investing more energy.

Besides, I couldn't have a healthy family life, teach 35 hours a week and grow the business. I needed to teach less. Well, this was what I told myself anyway.

The real truth is that I started waking up every day with worries of how I was going to pay the bills at the studio and at home. I dreaded seeing my students again, to have them need me, and worse, to take something from me when I felt depleted already with nothing left to give. I read books on business, metaphysics, and Buddhist philosophy. I talked to fellow entrepreneurs. And I fought to get my business partner to see that the business had gone astray and I needed to make a change, any change, even when I didn't know what that change was.

It was chaos and it was not working.

Our studio was a perplexing dichotomy of dedicated teachers and students, a thriving community with a first-rate reputation and endlessly taxing financial challenges. We had expanded too quickly: a common mistake, or so the MBA-holders and business journals told me. We had overextended ourselves. Our revenue was not matching our increasingly significant output. We had big dreams and small cash flow. We had done everything right in creating vision, community, and a safe and nurturing environment, but we were failing significantly in the business management department. Although my partner and I joke now about tag teaming our breakdowns, ultimately I felt responsible for it all.

I fell into the trap of so many overachievers who think things like, "I might as well attempt to balance the books, manage the staff, create the marketing campaigns, launch the website, teach and essentially, handle it all, because I can," and, "I'll do it all myself because it's likely I'll do it better, faster, and the right way," or, "If I don't know how to do something, I'll learn." Because that's what successful people do.

I believed we couldn't afford to pay someone with the financial and entrepreneurial expertise to step in, which only supported my folly. And so came one mistake in many: To work on my weaknesses (such as accounting and social media marketing) rather than play to my strengths (like building relationships, creating community and teaching—as much as I didn't want to admit it.)

Meanwhile, as I struggled to work on my weaknesses, teaching became unbearable. Inch by inch, I turned away from the true reason I started (to bring the joy of moving to others in the way I had experienced it my whole life) while telling myself that I had grown out of teaching. I hated every second of teaching for nearly a year and a half. I meditated, planned and tried everything I could think of to regain my balance. But all I could think of was how to get out.

How had I strayed so far from joyful teaching—from the passionate place from which my studio, my career, and my life, spurred? How had something so perfect and satisfying turned into something I longed to be rid of?

There appeared to be significant answers. The business had financially drained me to bankruptcy, and I blamed teaching. I was dissatisfied and exhausted, and I blamed teaching. I believed that teaching was the reason that after endless hours and years of giving 200 percent, I felt adrift and no closer to my financial goals or life dreams.

I told my partner that I wanted to sell my half of the business. And in her particular way, she said, "No. If you leave, the business will fail."

I felt like a hostage. My own guilt, shame and fear of failing was enough to make me stay on board—a destructive fuel.

I stayed on and taught less, thinking that I was doing the right thing. I was wrong. I continued to feel dissatisfied and wanted to teach even less often. I kept convincing myself that if I stayed and worked through the mess I would be happy again, and that I just needed some time and space to figure out how to love teaching again.

"If I did this or that or some other thing, I would feel better," I thought, just hoping that I was on the right path to relieve the mounting pressure. After all, I worked hard, so I should have been more successful, satisfied and compelled to keep it all going, right?

Ah, but there's more to this story than struggle alone. What about all that my work had brought me? What about the stuff I still loved about teaching and the work I had done for so long? What about the person I had become since I began teaching ten years ago? What about all the future might hold? This was not the end.

I was walking through the flames, at the pivotal part of every story where the classic hero (you and me and the guy on his laptop sitting next to me) is tempted to quit, blame, and let it all consume her or him. Now I see this part of my career as the true beginning. What is that silly thing "they" say: "What doesn't kill you makes you stronger?" Yes, well…sometimes you wonder.

The section below: "How To Create and Sustain a Satisfying Teaching Life: Five Essential Steps " is the result of my walk through this seemingly massive fire. I have walked through many more fires since then (with some currently peeking up on the horizon) and now I realize that fires are to be expected and we can count on them to change us.

So we move forward. We make hard choices and try to keep our heart at the center of those choices. We look at how much of our suffering is of our own making (my bet is on nearly 100%) and we make an effort to change those things that we can, while counting the many, many blessings we undoubtedly have. We put our expectations a little lower on the hierarchy of priorities and practice letting go.

Here's the thing I often hear myself saying when the next fire is about to ignite: "But it's not supposed to be this way!" Then I ask myself, 'what way should it be?' I am reminded of one of my favorite teachers, Byron Katie, who says that if it *is* happening it *should* be happening simply because it *is*. I cannot change what *is* happening, no more than I can change how gravity works.

Do not mistake this concept as defeatist or nihilistic—it isn't. It is just making friends with reality. In doing so, we can face our fears, demons and find our own motivation. We can reconnect with our strengths, learn how to keep it simple, know what we want and need, and learn to let go.

Today, I have reconnected with my teaching heart and rekindled my passion. But I've had to allow my path to change and my inspiration to be different from what it was 15 years ago.

I've allowed my needs, desires, and myself to change. And I've found that the act of letting go of my expectations and facing my fears gives me permission to clearly see something new blossoming.

And so I find myself here, with you and happy. I invite you to discover or rekindle what is at the heart of your teaching and how to integrate your inner self and your core values into every aspect of what you teach. I invite you to create a teaching life that is sustainable and joyful.

5
HOW TO CREATE & SUSTAIN
A SATISFYING TEACHING LIFE
FIVE ESSENTIAL STEPS

THERE ARE FIVE STEPS essential to building a solid and resilient foundation for our teaching careers. Revisited often these practices are powerful tools for sustaining lasting success.

1. Keep it simple.
2. Create a vision from your core commitments.
3. ALWAYS play to your strengths.
4. Identify and face your demons, fears, and motivations.
5. Practice letting go.

KEEP IT SIMPLE

Whether you own a studio or teach in someone else's, one thing applies to us all: how we nurture and evolve our teaching selves is a crucial part of our success. So how do we create an authentic, lasting and meaningful teaching career? By establishing contentment, deep satisfaction, life purpose, service and contribution. Money aside, this is about staying true to what is in our hearts when faced with demons, the inevitability of failure and fear—that ambiguous, nightmarish, renegade emotion.

One thing I've learned in more than a decade of owning my own business, and many more years of teaching, is that when in doubt it's best to keep it simple. This the best piece of advice

I can get or give. The urge or seeming necessity to make things complicated is massive and strong, like the pull of a large planet. Every time the idea of adding more begins to take form, step back and give yourself extra time and space to consider the true value of making things more complex.

Whether it's creating more services by adding packages, new programs, more teachers, a bigger space, a business partner or anything else you might be tempted to do, these additions will always equate to an exponential amount of work (and requisite resources).

That is not to say you should always say, "no" to expansion. Sometimes it's best to say, "yes." And sometimes it's better to say, "no" but you say, "yes" anyway. Other times, you will have no choice, and that is okay. In the end, however, no matter how you grow or expand, remember to keep it simple.

How to Keep it Simple:

1. Make sure your students can see to the HEART of what you offer. Don't let your growth mask the intent of your offer; growth should always align with your deepest values, both personally and professionally.
2. ALWAYS make it easy for your students to say YES to any program or service you offer.
3. The more choices you offer, the more likely people are to make NO CHOICE at all. So instead of offering students six ways to pay, 25 different class packages and eight different kinds of classes, streamline by giving them two ways to pay, four packages, and two types of classes.

4. Technology should always ENHANCE your service, NEVER detract from it (as it can so often end up doing.) For example, ask yourself, "How will my students benefit from Facebook, Twitter or using a QR code?"

5. CONSISTENCY is key. Even as you change the features offered through your business or teaching, be sure to maintain the benefits of what your students have come to expect (like inclusiveness or dependability). That way, change will feel natural and fluid because it will still reflect the values at the core of your work.

CREATE A VISION FROM YOUR CORE COMMITMENTS

There is no way to know exactly what the future may bring, even if we've worked in the corporate world, owned a business, or been teaching for 25 years. Any assurances we have come from understanding our purpose in life and ourselves. This requires not only reflection as we begin to teach, but constant self-inquiry as our business grows and changes.

What happens when we jump from simply being a teacher—fresh, inspired, happy and excited about our work—to business owner? How do we take what's most important to us and infuse it with our business? These questions might sound complex and even a bit heavy, but if you know where to look, arriving at the answers can be easy. If you can be honest and steadfast, these answers will be truly powerful.

The first question you must ask is:

What are my deepest-held values and commitments, not only

as a teacher, but as a person? Does, or will, my business reflect these values and commitments?

Core Commitments

No doubt you have had people tell you that creating a vision and a mission for your business is crucial. This is true —but how do you do that without clarity of your underlying beliefs? Likely you won't create a vision that withstands the trials of a changing business or one that reflects your true self. It's crucial to investigate why you make the choices you do.

I was introduced to the term "core commitments" from yoga and mindfulness teacher Sally Kempton (*Yoga Journal,* May 2009). These types of commitments, she writes, are different because they "can with-stand any amount of chaos and remain in place even when your external commitments are dissolving around you." They are a reflection of your values, principles and intentions. Once ferreted, they become an impenetrable foundation of a value-driven business.

For example, some of my core commitments are:
- To build community
- To be ethical and honest
- To be generous
- To offer assistance when others are in need
- To be creative and open to change
- To be compassionate and facilitate compassion in others

PERSONAL INVENTORY

What's at Your Core? — Questions to Ask Yourself

Consider the following questions to hone in on your core commitments:

1. What qualities in culture, art, nature, other people and the human experience inspire you?

2. What type of reward or outcome gives you the greatest joy in your work and in your life?

3. On what things are you unwilling to compromise when you are forced to make a change? For example: if you have to change jobs, are you willing to take a new position that is not creative, or doesn't allow you to spend much time with your family?

4. When you look back at your life what are some common threads? What have you consistently sought out in order to feel content or happy?

5. What situations, places, activities or actions make you feel like you are totally present, in the flow and energized? What qualities did these places, activities or situations possess to make you feel so good? What were you focused on in these moments?

You may also consider situations in which you have found yourself compromised or going against what feels right. Explore the circumstances and think about what you would do differently. Ask yourself, "Did my behavior or decision making align with my core commitments?" Looking at our mistakes can be the most profound way of understanding what's really important to us. Sometimes we don't know how important a particular value is until we've taken the wrong road. ————●

Make Them Real — Write Them Down

At some point you must not only muse over these things, but also make them real, substantive, and tangible. Make a list. Whether you write it at the top of your business plan, in a journal or on a piece of paper you post in your studio, you should be able to look at your core commitments often. If these commitments are constantly brought to your attention, your business will more likely reflect them—and not just in a vague or occasional way, but in a purposeful, consistent way in which all aspects of your business (from your website, to your business cards, to how you hire your staff, and how you treat your landlord) are affected and in sync.

Now that you know what lies at the core of your teaching and how you want to conduct business, you can construct a clear and concise plan for both. If you own a studio and have other teachers who work for you, either as employees or independent contractors, ask the members of the group to create a common vision as well as individual ones. This can be very powerful, as it gives everyone ownership of the work that has been co-created, not dictated. It takes energy and dedication from all of you, after all, to make the endeavor truly successful.

ALWAYS PLAY TO YOUR STRENGTHS

> *"My biggest challenge as a new teacher is that I have to remember that it's OK not to know everything. I just have to represent myself honestly, keep my students happy & safe, and continue to learn!"*
>
> —JO BRADEN, PILATES TEACHER

Somewhere along the line (between the first class I taught in that Hawaiian gym and now), I realized the value in saying, "I don't know." And I find I keep coming back to it. It allows me to practice starting over and offers me a chance to recognize that I have so much still to learn.

Recognizing our weaknesses can be one of our greatest strengths. It gives us the opportunity to be curious, creative and compassionate, which in turn maintains our ability to empathize with our students and guide them. This is crucial to our success and to our humility.

But here's the twist: While I am a strong advocate of being aware of the areas in which I can improve (in both my teaching and myself), getting better at what I'm already good at (and what comes naturally) can yield more sustainable and satisfying results than when working endlessly to improve a weakness that I have no aptitude or spark for whatsoever!

When we leverage our natural talents, we feel good and in the flow, resulting in greater successes and contentment. When we spend all of our time lamenting that we "should" be better at something, or be working hard to change our weaknesses to strengths, our efforts will often result in dissatisfaction and frustration. (Be forewarned: Skill is different from talent. Skill is like learning to hold a hammer and hit a nail, whereas talent requires an innate ability to use the hammer with coordinating speed, accuracy, rhythm and planning. Where skill is linear, talent is multi-dimensional.)

Why choose to waste our valuable time and creative energy by forcing our faults into assets? Why not get clear about what we love and what we feel compelled to do? If we're clear about where our talents lie, we can allow that to fuel our fire and lead us ahead.

The Do's and Don'ts of Building Your Strengths

DO: Attend to bad habits that reflect poorly on your teaching.

For example: saying "um" between every word or calling your students "guys" when they are not.

DON'T: Try to change every bad habit at once.

Instead, try to take small steps and acknowledge one bad habit at a time, being aware that a change in one habit can make a huge difference in your life and teaching. Besides, one bad habit is much less daunting to tackle when isolated and seen on its own.

DO: Watch other teachers.

Learn what their talents are and how they use them. Find out the reasons they do what they do. Discovering the "why" will inform and evolve your own teaching.

DON'T: Mimic another brilliant teacher.
Using his or her style will not resolve all of your teaching challenges. Although mimicry is an appropriate tool for learning, blindly emulating another teacher won't show you the true nature of your talents.

DO: Work on identifying your natural talents and find better ways to use them.
For example: You love anatomy and have a knack for it, go with it! Set yourself apart by being the "Anatomy Geek!"

DON'T: Try to keep up with other teachers by forcing skills that you may not be qualified to do or ready to utilize.
For example, if you work with another teacher who is great at assessing leg alignment, don't try to be great at it RIGHT NOW too. Learn from other teachers, ask them questions and add the findings to your repertoire, but ultimately, stay focused on your innate talent.

WHAT TO DO

Enhance your natural talents. Be mindful of which "bad habits" you can address without trying to change your weaknesses into strengths by:

- Making a list of your strengths and weaknesses. Be honest, but not overly critical.
- Choosing one strength and one weakness, then generate some ideas on how to work them in your teaching.

Find ways to exploit your strengths. Be mindful of your weaknesses without trying to "fix" them.

- Asking a colleague to make a list of all the things he or she appreciates about your teaching. Then highlight the things that feel exciting and natural to you, and focus on accentuating them.
- Asking a fellow teacher (or someone whose opinion you value) to observe your teaching and give both positive and constructive feedback.
- Making a point of working on that feedback for a week or month and invite fellow teachers back to observe your progress.

IDENTIFY AND FACE YOUR DEMONS, FEARS, AND MOTIVATIONS

Why face our fears and demons? What do they have to do with being an effective teacher? Well, perhaps nothing at first, but fears and demons inevitably surface at some point in every relationship, including the one we have with our work.

Demons

> "Each has its lesson; for our dreams in sooth, come they in shape of demons, gods, or elves, are allegories with deep hearts of truth that tell us solemn secrets of ourselves."
>
> —HENRY TIMROD, POET

I think of demons as those eccentricities, neuroses, bad habits, or other ineffective patterns we take from one situation to the next. Demons can be our tendency to judge, blame, play the martyr, micromanage or not face hard realities.

How do I beat my demons? I make friends with them. To try to banish them or defeat them would take a magnitude of firepower that I and most of us do not possess. So I just keep them in my sights. I know their names, their favorite flavor of ice cream and how they like to push my buttons. Because I have followed the steps below and have been willing to see my faults and follies over time, I know most of my demons well. And because I can feel them arise, many of my demons no longer have the power to sidetrack me or drag me down a path of self-doubt. Even better, they no longer stand between me and wise, thoughtful action. When my demons start to act up, I simply recognize that they don't have to be the only ones with opinions. I am always free to make a better choice with my demons exposed.

Simple Suggestions — How to Recognize and Get to Know Your Demons

1. **Be honest with yourself.** Don't be afraid to admit that you have faults, have more to learn or have messed things up. If you're at a different place on your path than others you admire, simply accept it. It's okay, truly. Knowing ourselves, both good and bad, in joy and in sorrow, in light and in darkness is the only way to move ahead.

2. **Identify, name and expose your demons.** One way to do this is by using humor. Like many, I've carried a lot of self-doubt. But at some point in my mid-twenties, I drew a crazy caricature of my self-doubt and named her "Spaz." I pinned her on the wall and there she lived, front-and-center, a total freak with black spiky hair. She was someone I could stick my tongue out at and tell to go away. So name your demons—draw them, journal about them, make a dartboard out of their faces. Use your imagination and expose them using any method that feels good and fun.

3. **Forgive yourself when your demons take charge.** Clean up any messes they made and know that it may happen again.

4. **Do your best** to consider your demons when making any major decision in life and work. Wherever you go, your demons go too.

Fear

We can treat fear much in the same way as we do our demons. No use in trying to get rid of fear; it's better to just name and face it. When you are comfortable with being uncomfortable, you take the power out of fear.

Sometimes we can equate fear with risk. When we know we are taking a risk, we feel fear—fear for what we might lose, for what we might not gain and of looking the fool in the process. Fear is just another emotion. It comes and it goes. Ultimately it never stays.

Fear makes you know you are alive. It tells you that you are doing something outside your safety zone. It's proof that you are on the ride, not sitting on the sidelines. When it comes to creating a healthy outlook for fear, here's the bottom line:

You will grow and evolve no matter what choice you make in the face of fear. You will either discover that you are more afraid then you thought, and will stay where you are and gain insight, or you will discover that you have courage and will move forward, and gain insight.

> "For all of the most important things, the timing always sucks. Waiting for a good time to quit your job? The stars will never align and the traffic lights of life will never all be green at the same time. The universe doesn't conspire against you, but it doesn't go out of its way to line up the pins either. Conditions are never perfect. 'Someday' is a disease that will take your dreams to the grave with you. Pro and con lists are just as bad. If it's important to you and you want to do it 'eventually,' just do it and correct course along the way."
>
> —TIMOTHY FERRISS, AUTHOR, *THE FOUR HOUR WORK WEEK*

Motivation

It is easy to be overwhelmed by the sheer volume of the Pilates Method, especially in the beginning. Even after years of teaching, we can quickly get lost in the adventures of learning new techniques and modalities, which can muddy our effectiveness as teachers and begin to pull us away from our true and most effective teaching nature. In those moments, knowing a lot can mean very little. It is crucial that we are able to distill our knowledge into effective tools and skills for our students, or we will begin to drift. No matter where you are in your career, it's important to examine why you do what you do and what motivates you to teach.

WHAT TO DO

Spend a few minutes jotting down some of your thoughts once every few months or even weeks. This will help you get clear on what motivates you when you feel lost or tethered. Ask yourself:

- Why did I start teaching?
- What is my greatest hope for my teaching?
- What is my greatest hope for my students?
- Who are my mentors, gurus and sources of inspiration?
- What qualities do my inspirers have that I would like to cultivate in myself?
- What qualities would I like to cultivate in my students? ●

When in doubt, look at your core commitments (see Chapter 2) to see what keeps you grounded. To gain perspective on moving ahead, think about your vision and why you started teaching.

Cori Martinez, owner of Asha Yoga, in Sacramento, CA, and teacher trainer said recently, "When I feel uninspired, I know that I have all I need to get back on track. All I have to do is reconnect with why I fell in love with yoga in the first place— it's all there and I know what to do. I just have to do it."

PRACTICE LETTING GO
(AND DON'T TAKE IT PERSONALLY)

We've all walked out of a class or session at some point and felt like we did a shoddy job. We carry that feeling of totally "sucking it" with us for the rest of the day, week, or even weeks or months. We've also all had those moments when a student decided they weren't going to come back or they just stopped showing up and we immediately imagine it was because of something we did.

This is not just a curse of the novice teacher. This sense of doubt and blame can arise anytime in our teaching career. And it will continue to arise if we don't learn how to face and dissolve it. Sometimes, self-doubt stems from a lack of self-confidence or from a deep-seated desire to be praised or liked. Other times, it can come from the need to control every situation and every outcome. And still for others, it can arise as a preoccupation with achieving a specific goal or result—of meeting set expectations just for the sake of meeting them alone (as if by doing so, we fulfill our reason for teaching).

There are Two Components of Letting Go

1. Take responsibility for our own actions and interactions, never for those of the other person.

How someone else responds in a situation is not about us, and ultimately, is none of our business. Too many times we absorb not only how we behave or perform, but how the other person behaves as well. As if we could be solely responsible for the things that anyone else might do! We can't and it's madness to think otherwise.

We should not take our role as teacher lightly or be flippant about how others feel. However, when we act with professionalism, integrity, and honesty (and we should strive for this), then we can know that we have done our absolute best. And if it is not enough? Then it's not enough from the other person's end.

2. Don't let whether we fail or succeed determine our success, or more importantly, our satisfaction. This comes back to our core commitments and motivations (discussed in Chapter 2).

If we are teachers because we always want to get results, always make a profound impact, always get it right, then I've got some bad news: We will be disappointed. And being disappointed is no way to spend a teaching life (or any part of life for that matter). If we are teachers because giving fills us up and because we truly believe that what we teach can make an impact, then just showing up with that knowledge and intention is enough. We can let go of everything else.

I am not, by any means, saying that this is easy or that we are capable of this kind of response all the time. But I am saying that when we are clear about why we teach, it becomes easier to stay connected to what really brings us joy. This joy reconnects us to the original and inspired reason we chose to teach in the first place. The rewards of teaching do not hinge on whether others endlessly sing our praises or always do what we think is best.

Not taking things personally and letting go is a relief. Mostly, it gives us the space to be great at what we do. And I can't recommend it enough.

6

CULITIVATING GENEROSITY
THE KEY TO BUILDING A THRIVING, MEANINGFUL
& SUCCESSFUL STUDIO ENVIRONMENT

"If you hold your hand closed, nothing good can come in. The open hand is blessed, for it gives in abundance, even as it receives."

—BRIDGET "BIDDY" MASON, FIRST AFRICAN AMERICAN
LANDOWNER, REAL ESTATE MOGUL, PHILANTHROPIST

"YOU'RE BLOWING MY MIND RIGHT NOW," is not what you would expect to hear from someone attending a workshop on how to give an introductory session. However, in any given teacher training, an all-too common scenario ensues: the students and teacher have reviewed the teaching formats, variations and suggested exercise modifications; they've combed through the relevant paperwork, discussed the ins and outs of assessment and studied the manual. But at the end of the day the student teachers want to know how they're going to navigate real-life scenarios:

What are they to do when faced with integrating and retaining a student? What does it mean to be the expert? What does generosity have to do with making a recommendation for practicing Pilates? And what outcome should a teacher aim for when trying to create a plan for his or her students to practice?

Oftentimes, teachers haven't thought much beyond the intricacies of teaching the exercises or of being the technician.

And naturally so—as mentioned in chapter one, the internal and personal aspects of teaching life lies beyond the how-tos and outside of the scope of where most teacher trainers and programs are willing or able to venture.

We don't talk much about the elements of creating relationships, building trust with students or holding to a larger vision of how to teach – especially at the onset. There's too much else to do and to learn. We shield our new teachers from overly complex relationship skills and tools because we don't want to overwhelm them.

To the detriment of these teachers in training, we assume that these things are either inherent or out of our scope of practice as teacher trainers. But nothing could be more within our scope. We are in the business of building relationships. And lasting relationships are made on a foundation of giving.

TEACHING AS SERVICE

Teaching, as lasting and meaningful work, is primarily an act of service. When we are truly invested in what's best for our students, then teaching is a vehicle not only for generosity, but for contributing to the bigger picture—changing the world. We teach, run a business or own a studio not just because it serves our ego or is an expression of our entrepreneurial urges, but because our work is truly about making someone's life better. Teaching from the perspective of service immediately puts us in a generous state of mind.

"Never stop inspiring others and contributing to the world," writes Michael Carroll, in his book, *The Mindful Leader*. As one of his 30 reminders for creating truly meaningful work and leadership, Carroll speaks directly about our underlying purpose. If we are committed to contributing and inspiring, then we are guided by what's best for the whole, not just ourselves.

In the goings on of our daily routine, we are faced with any number of opportunities to be thoughtful and to adhere to our greater commitment. In the Pilates studio, we make endless decisions about which exercises or poses to use, what kind of program or teachers to recommend, what to charge, what policies to implement and other logistics that either line up with our greater commitment or do not.

Where do *you* stand? The good news is that it's pretty easy to tell. When we are blindly motivated by what will be best for us, we feel badly (sometimes sooner than later, but it comes around in the end). We also lose students and employees, our profits drop or worse, we end up hating or feeling indifferent about what we do.

If we are on track, at the very *least* we show up excited to offer our teaching. Inevitably this leads to a staff that feels supported and inspired, students that can't wait to come in, and growing profits. This leads to success with the **"R" word— retention!**

GENEROSITY AT WORK

How to turn the most challenging situations into acts of generosity and achieve student retention.

The Scenario

You've just completed an introductory session and you see that the student would be best served by coming in twice a week for five weeks, but you will be out of town part of that time. You know the student needs consistency, because staying motivated has been a challenge for her in the past.

The Generous Solution

Offer to schedule her next appointment with a fellow teacher instead of trying to make it work with your upcoming schedule.

The Retention Win

Since the beginning of a practice is the most crucial time for a new student, and your ultimate intention is to make people excited about Pilates and to help provide a significant change in his or her life, it's best to put the student's needs before your own and schedule them with another teacher. This not only feels better for both teacher and student, it significantly increases the probability of retaining that student long term.

The Scenario

You've just completed 10 weekly sessions with a new student and he is progressing well. You know that finances are a concern for him, but you've also just lost another student and would really like to keep this new student at the higher, private-session price point. It wouldn't be a detriment for the student to complete 10 more private sessions, but you see he is excited about gaining more strength. Group classes would allow the student to achieve his goals, while giving him twice as much access to classes (and at the same price to boot).

The Generous Solution

Enroll the student in group classes that works best for his schedule (even if it's with another teacher) and let him know you'll check in with him in 2–3 weeks to see how he is progressing.

The Retention Win

The student will have to opportunity to practice Pilates twice as often and will see that you have his best interest at heart. After all, you and your studio are most committed to students practicing for the long run, not just for as long as it benefits you.

The Scenario

You have a relatively new student who is consistently asking you to accommodate her ever-changing needs by rearranging sessions and coming in on your days off. She is constantly comparing you to other teachers and questioning your decisions. The kicker? She's often late for her sessions. You have been flexible so far because you are building your practice and you want her to stay. Yet, you leave every session feeling badly. Other students and teachers notice the negativity this student contributes to the studio's atmosphere.

The Generous Solution

You either recommend that the student try a different teacher who might better suit her schedule and needs, or refer her to the studio down the street. (Generosity toward yourself should not be under-emphasized as a key aspect of your contribution!)

The Retention Win

When you respect your needs and boundaries you inspire employees to do the same, ensuring a happy and consistent staff and self. Plus, referring the student elsewhere leaves room for other new students who are better suited to your business.

PERSONAL INVENTORY

How To Maintain Generosity

Ask yourself the following questions:

1. Do I refer students easily and readily to other teachers or studios?
2. Am I willing to turn a student away if I see he or she needs something other than Pilates or if I know I won't be able to serve him or her well (think: conflict of character etc.)?
3. Do I create goals and programs that truly fit my students' needs even if it takes them away from me directly?
4. Is service a part of my business model (this pertains to both studio owners and individuals)? Do I contribute my time and efforts to support a charity or cause?
5. If I'm an employee or teacher in someone else's studio, am I willing to participate, support and contribute even when it's not easy? If not, why? What motivates this decision? Note: *If you are not, perhaps this is the time to examine the lack of generosity in the studio or employer. Are your underlying commitments being reinforced by where you've decided to teach?

WHAT TO DO

Make a list of areas in which you feel you are in need of improvement. Begin to look at where you are not being generous and explore why. For instance, maybe finances are tight and you feel like you need to keep every student that walks in the door, even if he or she is the biggest jerk you've ever met and is bad for studio morale. Perhaps you will do *anything* to get a student to sign up because you really need to make rent this month.

Start to peel back the layers and see how being generous might make you fearful. Do you generally feel afraid of not having enough whether financially, emotionally, or physically? Are you fearful of taking risks and putting yourself out there to be seen? Are you concerned with providing for yourself monetarily and fear that giving more to those who work for you will detract from what you yourself can have?

Now think: "What's the worst that could happen if I begin to respond *rather than react* and make decisions based on inspiring others and on generosity?" At the very least, you start to feel better about yourself and your work, and it will shine through to everything you do. And guess what? People are attracted to others who are confident and feel good about themselves. The best thing (*and likely thing*) to happen is that your students will make honest and clear decisions from the outset and opt to stay with you because your heart is in it and theirs is too. ————●

7

TAKING STUDENT RETENTION TO THE MOON
SIMPLE, ACTIONABLE STEPS TO GUIDE YOU NOW & DOWN THE ROAD

FIVE COMMON CHALLENGES IN KEEPING STUDENTS

1. Not knowing where to start
2. Not preparing in advance by having a student retention plan or tracking system in place
3. Being flaky or inconsistent
4. Not following up with a student who has been absent for more than a few weeks because you feel ashamed or at fault
5. Not giving new students a reason to stay for the long run, and as a result, they don't even know you *want* them to stay

FIVE SIMPLE STRATEGIES FOR KEEPING STUDENTS

1. Ask students for feedback.

This is a concept a friend of mine is always repeating (and is one of the only things he says he learned in business school): "Follow the ants." Basically, let your students guide you. Ask them what they want and how to make their experience even better. Then find a way to address those things. This will provide happier, more satisfied students. Don't spend time *imagining* what new or current students want or what *you* would want if you were in their position. The best possible outcome in these situations will leave you simply hoping your *imagined* needs for your students align with their *actual* needs. Mind-reading is not typically going to work out as well for us as it did for *Twilight's* Edward Cullen. Instead, cut out the middleman. Stop pretending you know what students are looking for and JUST ASK!

WHAT TO DO

- Print or email surveys after a student's first visit or initial trial period (depending on what you offer).
- Survey your entire student population twice a year.
- Ask for and engage in face-to-face feedback after a student has had the chance to build some trust and experience with you.

2. Make a plan to REALLY know your business and your students.
A little forethought and preparation go a long way. It is so much more effective to know what's coming and simply address it than to scramble when things are falling apart.

How do you prepare for an unpredictable future? Review your survey results and make a list of situations and scenarios in which students get stuck or fall off track. For example: What do most students struggle with when committing to a plan? Is it motivation, scheduling, family pressures, self-doubt and/or pain? Or at what point in their practice do students typically get deterred, unmotivated, or distracted? Is it in the first two weeks, at the end of their 10 private sessions, or transitioning between private and group instruction?

WHAT TO DO

Set aside a time at the beginning of the year and make a strategic plan for how you will regularly attend to the student concerns or struggles you've listed above. For instance, you might schedule a bi-monthly postcard to be sent to all students who haven't come in for a month or more.

Or you might start a "call campaign" in which you make a list of students you need to touch base with, and reach out to those students, asking fellow teachers to take turns making those calls. Call campaigns are a great way to engage both new and long-term students.

Once a month, look ahead on your calendar to note holidays and other approaching events that would cause students to stop coming in (such as Thanksgiving or summer plans). This will help mitigate anticipated drop-off and serve as a call to action for you. If you provide students with rewards for staying committed during busy times, they'll be less likely to slough off. The best motivation I can give myself for keeping ahead of the slow times of year is to remember how stressful it is when I'm *not* prepared. I have little notes posted on my strategic plan and calendar that say: "If you don't prepare, life is going to get REAL hard!" This helps remind me to revisit my plan and calendar once a month. I hate to say it, but the threat of something bad happening is often a greater motivator than the promise of something great.

Next, make a plan for the unpredictable circumstances that students often use as excuses for not returning to the studio after a brief absence, such as troubles finding childcare, an out-of-town work conference, a field-trip, a family visit, a cold or other small reasons to miss a week or two. If these interruptions stretch into three, four or five-month periods, it becomes *essential* to reach out and invite your students back in. Often, the grind of life takes students away from the studio, causing them to feel embarrassed about not returning. Sometimes we simply need to extend ourselves to them, letting them know they are missed and reminding them that the work they were doing is valuable. ————————————————————●

CHECKLIST

Getting Your Head in the Game

Check your calendar every six months for the following (and inevitable) student-retention speed bumps:
- Busy times of year (vacation seasons, holidays, school schedules).
- Different phases in new and ongoing students' practice (at 2 months, 6 months and so on).
- Times when a student has been absent for more than 2 weeks.

- After a student has suffered an illness or returned from a vacation.
- Review and, if necessary, adjust your own planned absences. Guarantee uninterrupted service for your students by finding another teacher to cover for you when you're gone.
- If you are going to have a substitute teach for you when you are out of the studio, it's best to find a way to encourage your student(s) to come in no matter what. (Students sometimes choose not to come in at all, rather than to work with a sub. It is our responsibility to prime them for working with multiple teachers or offer other class options in our absence.) ———————●

3. Be consistent and follow through.

There are two ways in which being flaky and inconsistent can set you back. First, students will feel neglected—like they're not a priority, you don't need their business, and you don't have their best interest at heart. Second, they will never know what to expect from you or from your business and therefore won't depend on you or trust you to guide them.

Students want a flawless and predictable experience. "They don't want to see behind the curtain," as one of my teachers recently remarked, which means you need to be steady—not only in the service you provide, but *how* you provide it. Always make good on what you are selling. For example, if you have a referral plan, a procedure for following up with new students, or any other policy or system, keep it all consistent.

CHECKLIST

How to Inspire Consistency in Your Student Base

Make sure you do everything possible to maintain your student base by trying the following:

- Keep it simple!! Enact manageable and basic offers and policies that lend themselves to consistency for students and staff.
- Do everything in your power not to cancel classes. If you have staff, make sure they know the protocol for getting classes covered and keep teacher cancelations as close to zero as possible.
- Make each student feel equally appreciated and treasured. If you send one student a birthday note, do it for every other student as well.
- Make it a "best practice" policy. A best practice is a go-to protocol, which aligns with your vision (and core commitments) and features tried-and-true operating procedures that get you the absolute best results in any given area of your work. Best practices can be applied to teaching, running a studio, conducting business, communicating, and more. If you run a studio make sure your whole staff (or anyone you have assisting you) is on board with how to execute these practices.

4.   Make it personal.

Don't be afraid to reconnect with a student, even when you feel like he or she will never return. Do the same in times when you feel you could have or *should have* done more for a student. Those who have made a commitment to you once are more likely to do it again—even if they've begun to waver in their practice. And if a student feels ashamed for having dropped off the face of the earth, your friendly encouragement can make all the difference in getting that student back in the studio and on track. Making a real connection with each student works both when your student or *you* have gone astray.

Follow-up or reach out to your students at different phases of their practice and do so in a way that feels authentic to you. Hand-written notes or phone calls usually work best for adding that personal touch. Emails work too, but make sure your student prefers email; never send a bulk email. Remember: make it personal.

CHECKLIST

How to Maintain Student Relationships

To stay connected and sustain professional and mutually beneficial relationships with your students, reach out to them every three to six months in the following ways:

- Follow up with students with notes and phone calls.
- Send personal birthday notes or customer loyalty coupons to your students (and remember to include your entire student-base.)

- Make connecting with your students a priority. Keep in mind that checking in with a student to find out how he or she is doing is not a sales pitch; it's discovering whether there is a new way that you can support them in their practice.

5.   Be the expert who sets a clear course.

When new students walk in to your space, they do so with the expectation that *you* are the expert who knows how the practice works. They need you to guide them, tell them how to practice and make recommendations that will support their needs. When you are unclear, your students become unclear. And wavering students will inevitably seek guidance elsewhere.

Know how you want students to use your services. That is, have a structure in place for exactly how students should best begin, progress, advance and achieve their goals in your studio according to your programming.

Think of this as guiding them through "The Most Successful Way to Practice" in your studio. Articulate long-term objectives for your students by creating a precise path of progression (or a detailed map of how to practice) using components that have proven successful for other students and the studio.

This means you have to do your homework and analyze what has worked and what hasn't, what fits your studio programming and what facilitates the greatest success for your business. Know how you want your students to practice by letting them know what is possible from the beginning and how you are going to help them achieve those goals. Get them excited about in-studio achievement!

CHECKLIST

How to Show Expertise and Set Student Objectives

Give students structure and confidence in your overall teaching and recommendations by doing the following:

- From the outset, give students a step-by-step explanation of how your services work and of how you take care of your students.
- Invite students to begin their practice by making a firm recommendation for how to practice based on their needs.
- Explain to students that their goals can be achieved after 1 month, 6 months, or 6 years of practice if they stick to their commitment.
- Help students become healthy, pain-free practitioners for the long run.

BONUS Strategy!

6. Offer Value: How to give more than you get and feel good about it.
Students are like any other customers—they want to know they are getting a good value. Look for ways to add something extra or special to your services, something no one else in your area offers.

CHECKLIST

Delight Your Customer with "The Extras"

Increase your services value by providing these simple perks:

- Give students monthly practice tips (in print or email).
- Send students follow-up emails with homework notes or tips for practicing on the road.
- Offer online resources to your students, such as an audio or video routine. (This doesn't have to be one of your own making—it could be a resource page of routines you love to do yourself.)
- Provide hot tea at the front door.
- Be creative.

8

FIVE SURE-FIRE TIPS TO AMPLIFY YOUR RETENTION PRACTICES

1. **Review your retention numbers every month.**

Look at which students stayed. Examine where those students started, how they are practicing now, and evaluate any other relevant circumstances (positive and negative) that might have effected their decision to continue practicing with you.

2. **Conduct a student survey.**

Believe it or not, semi-annual surveys do wonders. You may think you know your students, but do you really? Don't guess— know! Send a survey to all current students via email or print every six months or at the end of the year. Or try dividing your entire student list into two different surveys: active students (those who have been in to the studio in the past 12 months) and inactive students (those who haven't visited the studio in a year or more.) Be proactive and find out whether what you've been doing is working.

How and When to Survey

For best results when surveying your students about specific programs, changes you plan to implement or when drilling into certain aspects of your business, try to ask questions that are relevant to how students are using or experiencing this particular facet of your business. For instance, if you want to know how your new class packages are working, survey students just before they finish that package. If you want to know how your new introductory special is working, survey students after they have finished the special. (This is a great way to find out how the transition went from trial to a full-price package.) Opt to survey students at times when you think their feedback will be new and relevant to growing a service or other aspect of your business. When you consider these elements beforehand, a well-thought-out analysis will influence your timing and the questions you ask, making your surveys more precise and therefore garner more accurate results.

3.   Self-evaluate.

There are times when things may simply feel *off*, like when we have ebb in business or we feel unmotivated. Look at what's going on with honest eyes. Is there a new trend emerging with your students? Did you change something in your business? Are your students noticing a personal slump or change in your attitude that may cause them not to show up? Whenever you notice a rough spot, try to recognize it and make it an opportunity for positive change.

4.   Be willing to change course.

As your teaching and/or business grow and change, so should your approach. Make sure to evaluate how you are handling your student relationships when you change your priorities, commitments or even location. Ensure that any change you consider is consistent with your overall vision and core commitments—particularly when the shift directly effects interactions with your students.

Your students will be the first to know when something is different, especially when it feels at odds with what they are used to. Bottom line: when you notice things are not working out quite like you planned, don't ignore it—do something about it.

5. Stay true to yourself.

No matter how you go about maintaining students, the process should feel authentic. Stay grounded and on track with your core commitments by occasionally asking yourself whether you're feeling good about how you run your business. It is easy to follow someone else's advice, only to find that those things don't actually support what you are most committed to. Remember it's a work in progress because you're a work in progress.

9
DOES YOUR STUDIO HAVE HEART?

"There are hundreds of things teachers need to know in order to achieve greatness, many of which are discovered as needed."

—WILLIAM AYERS & RYAN ALEXANDER-TANNER,
"TO TEACH: THE JOURNEY, IN COMICS"

In my studio, we have a student break down in tears at least once a month. With significantly more frequency, we have students show up for sessions angry, distracted, worried, discouraged and sometimes bursting at the seams with excitement; every one of these instances is due to the remnants of life outside of the studio. It can be a lot to contend with, especially as we attempt to guide students into the stream of their sessions.

Not only are we confronted with the physical challenges, limitations or traumas of our students, but also with the underpinnings of their mental and emotional states. In order to keep ourselves healthy, focused and effective, we must be attentive to how we interact with our students, from the very first encounter we have with them.

In the following paragraphs we will look at how to create a healthy teacher-student relationship (which can be just as tough and complex to navigate as with any other relationship) by establishing clear values, setting boundaries and building trust and respect.

Perhaps we have an objective as to what we desire from the teacher-student relationship because we offer a specific service and we are familiar with the desired outcomes. But human interactions of any kind come with infinite and unexpected twists and turns. With a little forethought and clarity, we can better prepare ourselves to build lasting, healthy, goal-oriented and mutually rewarding relationships with our students, whatever their mood du jour.

First and foremost we should look at our foundation. What are our personal and professional values? For instance, do we consider our students "clients" or "students" primarily? This is something I have had to look at very recently and here's what I've had to ask myself: Am I most committed to teaching or running a business?

Teaching is the heart of what I do. But I also run a business. Unfortunately, when I slip into entrepreneur mode, I begin to think of my students as "clients." However, across the board, I am more committed to my role as a partner and a guide—someone whose motivations are driven by seeing progress and success. I want my students to see the bottom line, measured by how well they feel, *not* how much I can get them to pay. So, I choose the term "student." Obviously my choice to teach isn't strictly altruistic, and my financial bottom line *is* relevant, but I am happier and more focused on what inspires me in the context of "student" and teacher verses "client" and teacher.

How do you choose to view your customers: as "students" or "clients?" Why? Neither outlook is right or wrong. But our perspective does color our work and determine, in large part, how and why we make our choices.

What kind of demeanor do we want to project? Do we consider ourselves educators, service providers or both? What are our strengths and how do we use them to formulate our relationships? What do we need to keep balance in our work lives?

If we don't answer these questions, our impact and effectiveness are diminished, particularly in the face of challenging circumstances. For instance, a teacher friend of mine recently shared his own struggle with establishing respect and authority among his students. As a novice teacher he found himself making concessions for his new students to ensure they liked him and continued working with him. But granting these concessions made him feel uncomfortable. Further, he found that students he made allowances for were more likely to take advantage of him by being late, expecting unreasonable schedule changes and more.

PERSONAL INVENTORY

Look closely at what feels authentic to you in terms of the kinds of relationships you want to build in your work environment. Find a quiet place and sit for 15 minutes or so. Write down brief, off-the-cuff and honest answers to the following questions:

1. What are my personal and professional values?
2. What kind of demeanor do I want to project to my students and fellow staff?

3. What are my strengths and how do I use them to form my relationships?
4. What do I need to keep balance in my work life? ————●

WHAT TO DO

Chose a few of the previous questions that resonate with you most to answer in-depth.

It's important to write your responses down (not just think about them) so you can come back to them later. Your priorities (and therefore responses) will likely change over time. So if you don't capture them now, you may not be *aware* of when and how they change. Remaining unaware of our behavioral patterns will cause us to go astray and lead to compromising situations in our work. Our core commitments become the answers to most, if not all of the challenges we may face while teaching.

Once you've clarified your underlying values, it is easier to establish comfortable teaching boundaries that suit both your personality *and* your professional goals.

One of the most significant pitfalls for teachers is not knowing where our boundaries lie, or worse, having ambiguous boundaries between professional responsibility and personal investment. When we establish clear boundaries for ourselves, each action can be weighed and we can ask poignant and career-saving questions. Questions like: Is my getting to know a student (often an intimate and revealing process and an important part of earning trust) in line with my professional standards? Does my approach cultivate dedication and respect? When we know where we want to stand in our relationships, we can stay on track more effectively. ────────────────●

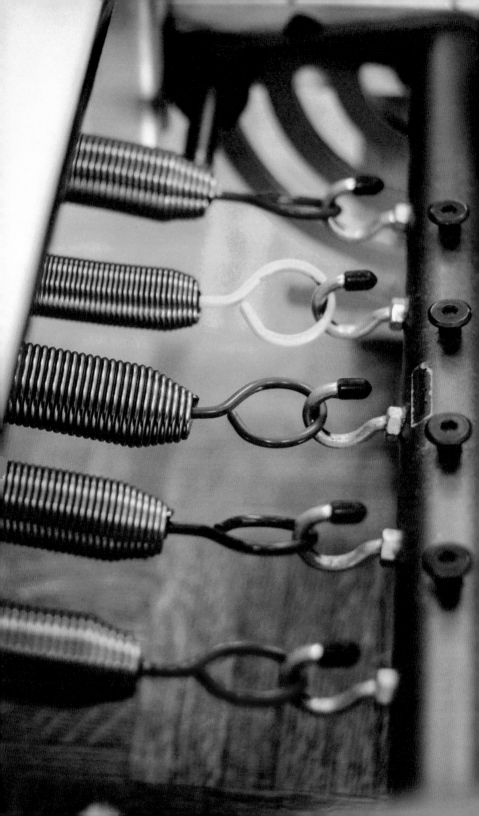

10
KEYS TO CULTIVATING HEALTHY IN-STUDIO RELATIONSHIPS

MASTER TEACHER CAROL APPEL, of Carol Appel's Pilates Plus Studio in Petaluma, California has been teaching for more than 25 years. Appel has addressed the challenges of student-teacher relationships time and again as a teacher trainer. She emphasizes how to manage these relationships in ways that manifest positive results for both teacher and student.

"Always focus on the client," Appel told me in a recent email. "The client is not our friend (despite the closeness that develops), and is not there to listen to the teacher's issues. The teacher is there to listen to the client's issues. In this business, the teacher is the motivator and should be wholly focused on servicing the client's needs. It is not a two-way street. As soon as the focus shifts to the teacher's need, the relationship has changed," Appel advises.

Because trust, rapport and understanding are such a large part of the teacher-student relationship in Pilates, it's easy to blur the edges of our relationships without even realizing it. We let our personalities come through in order to "relate" to the student and we share body stories in order to establish understanding. We create an atmosphere for students who are struggling physically or emotionally in an effort to keep them feeling safe. These interactions form bonds between a teacher and a student but can easily turn into opportunities for the teacher to rely on the student for reciprocation.

Recently, I spoke with a veteran teacher whose student made maintaining boundaries very difficult. After several sessions, the teacher realized that she had to take a more firm stance as to what was appropriate behavior during their session time. Although she faced the possibility of losing the student, she knew that in order to be an effective teacher, she had to draw a hard line between being congenial and friendly and getting the work done. Sometimes our students come to the studio for more than Pilates—they come looking for a place to be heard. These situations are equally important to navigate with thoughtfulness.

PERSONAL INVENTORY

Consider if, when, and how you do the following things when forging a teacher/student relationship:
1. Establish trust and mutual respect?
2. Enforce accountability?
3. Communicate in difficult situations?
4. Share personal details?
5. Establish time boundaries (starting/stopping on time and scheduling)?
6. Relay in-studio etiquette?
7. Establish a communication protocol for how students should contact you when you're outside the studio (or whether this is even appropriate)?

WHAT TO DO

NOTE: The exercises in this section are a bit meaty so take your time with them. Choose one that resonates with you and spend some time on it before you try the others. There's no rush. The longer you can work with one question, the greater insight you're bound to have. These exercises can also be used for the long run, as a way of checking in with yourself as time goes by.

Think of a recent new student and note how you set the stage for their first session or encounter with your service or studio. For example, did you ask "How are you today?" or "How is your body today?" Notice if what you say feels authentic and aligns with your core commitments. Are you asking the right questions and listening well to what the student needs?

You can also take a day to pay special attention to what you say and how you behave with different students. Write these things down to use for further reflection. Notice where you can make changes in both communication and your professional demeanor; such changes will create more solid and lasting relationships. Look for specific characteristics in teachers you admire and observe or ask how they handle situations you may be struggling with. You will find this work comes in very handy when managing student relationships gets sticky. ━━━━━●

WHAT TO DO

Make a list of areas in which you feel strong boundaries should be set, such as: the manner in which you greet a student, the mood you set as you start a session, in-session conversation or chatter, storytelling, personal sharing, cancelations, tardiness, communications outside of a session, or dress code. The list can span a wide range of elements from personal to practical. Consider your personality and teaching style, the type of environment you teach in and the goals you make with your students. Write these boundaries down and post them where you can see them regularly. Consider the questions from the **Personal Inventory** section above as examples of the ways in which boundaries can be set.

Many teachers stress the importance of establishing and tracking students' goals and achieving success in meeting these goals. As teachers, we must also be accountable to our students. When we make verbal and written agreements with our students, then we can demonstrate follow-through and provide consistent results. And when we achieve these results, we are more likely to develop trust and find greater success and ease in our work. This practice also serves as an avenue for engaging in clear communication at all times.

11
BACK TO THE BEGINNING: STARTING OVER

What kind of teacher do you want to be?

Are you any closer to finding out what kind of teacher you want to be? Are you any closer to knowing what lies beyond your ability to deliver repertoire and explain anatomy?

This is not a race. It's a true inner journey. There is no end or final resting place for becoming the ultimate version of ourselves as teachers or as people. Just yesterday I had to face another major hurdle in my ever-changing teaching path. Today, I sit here, writing, filled with trepidation as to how it will all come together—or if it will at all.

Not being able to see the outcome is always difficult. But not knowing can also be liberating. It is an indication that we have ventured someplace we haven't been. It tells us that we are moving forward, whether physically, emotionally, or psychologically. We are growing. Not knowing means we have decided to continue to build and change even though it is risky. And this book is meant for times when we feel uncertain or need direction.

You may not find that all the contents of *Moving Beyond Technique* are relevant at the same moment. You may not be able to relate to some of the scenarios just yet. But the insights and tools are here for you when you need them. Teaching is a work in progress. Be patient and enjoy the beautiful ups and downs. It all leads to a meaningful, joyful and authentic teaching life. You'll see. This is not the end. It's the beginning. It's a chance to start over…again, and again, and again.

12
MAKING IT STICK

What I want you to do is choose ONE THING (and only ONE) to do RIGHT NOW:

- **Talk to me** — Email me at chantill@skillfulteaching.com and let's get on the phone or Skype and figure out what you need most! I'm serious! *Are you?*

- **Get on my radar** — Sign up for the Skillful Teaching mailing list. Go to the website link below and get yourself on my radar. Being pinged (not obnoxiously but consistently) helps us stay connected to what's important. If you think I have something that you might benefit from, let's stay in touch!

- **Grab a free course** — At **skillfulteaching.com/online-courses** you will find (at the bottom of the page) a selection of very cool FREE courses that you are definitely going to want to dive into. ONE at a time though…

- **Jump into the next 28-Day Fulfilled & Successful Pilates Teacher Online Course** — I'm just going to come right out and say it…THIS is the ONE thing you should choose if you seriously want to make changes in your teaching and your life. Just saying… check it out. And it's the perfect segue between book and real-life implementation.

- **Go BIG** — Be mentored by me. Join my 12-month mentoring program. **The Engaged Teacher Roadmap Mentorship Program** is the most comprehensive post-certification support out there—hands down—that offers teachers serious results at ANY STAGE. For maximum support, community, technical continuing education, personal and professional development THIS is it. Go online to **skillfulteaching.com/mentoring-program** and find out more.

As I said in the beginning of this book, I'm here to help. Lean on me, ask me questions about your teaching, your business, your teachers, your education, your work and life balance, your values and commitments and purpose in life. That's what I'm here for. Give it to me. I'm ready when you are.

With love and gratitude,

Chantill

APPENDIX

1. Katie, Byron, page 24
2. Kempton, Sally, page 30
3. Braden, Jo, page 33
4. Timrod, Henry, page 37
5. Martinez, Cori, page 39
6. Ferriss, Timothy, page 40
7. Mason, Bridget "Biddy," page 45
8. Carroll, Michael, page 47
9. Ayers, William, page 69
10. Alexander-Tanner, Ryan, page 69
11. Appel, Carol, pages 74, 80

ACKNOWLEDGMENTS

I want to first acknowledge the endless support and love that my husband Carlos and family have provided me in this unexpected and brisk walk to authorhood. To my son Charlie and daughter Cydney, for keeping me in the moment and always focused on what is most important—my family. To my mother Constance, and father J.W., for their faith in me, and for giving me the best of themselves (accidentally and on purpose). To my sisters Anna and Amber (also the photographer who took all the wonderful images you see on and in this book), who consistently love me no matter how crazed I get and who keep me humble (even when it's unwanted.) To my darling friend, teaching partner, collaborator, and fellow adventure-seeker Cori Martinez, who is a constant source of hard truth and encouragement. To my friend and fellow entrepreneur Sean Daily, who assuaged my doubts that I could write a book. To my mentor, Carol Appel for giving me an unshakeable foundation and who keeps taking me deeper. To my former business partner Kristen Iuppenlatz Grech, who taught me so much about making it through difficult times and who has been a dear friend and confidant. And to my editor Erika Stalder, who prompted me to look more closely at every assumption, clarify every generalization, and make every word more powerful. With her expert help this book finally found its way.

ABOUT THE AUTHOR

CHANTILL'S TEACHING PHILOSOPHY: Be real. Don't fake it. Be able to say you don't know. Laugh at yourself. Extend compassion to yourself and your students. Enter in fully, every time, ready or not.

Chantill has been practicing Pilates for nearly 20 years, and teaching movement since 1990. She was a semi-professional contemporary dancer for many years while at first pursuing a career in journalism and later in the movement arts. In the past four years Chantill has combined both passions to create the educational company Skillful Teaching.

Through Skillful Teaching she combines her training and expertise as a movement teacher, meditation practitioner, anatomy geek, and creative entrepreneur to help guide teachers toward more fulfilling work and personal lives.

Chantill is a Pilates Method Alliance Certified teacher who studied both through the PhysicalMind Institute and with second generation Master Teacher Carol Appel, a direct descendant of Romana Kryzanowska. She is a Balanced Body Faculty member and Director of Education and Mentoring at Pilates Collective in Northern California, a studio she co-founded in 2006. As we speak she is also working on her second book *The Art of Skillful Teaching: The Ultimate Resource Guide For Movement Teachers.*

Chantill lives in Northern California with her husband, son and daughter, and teaches throughout the United States and Mexico.